THE SHORT FALL FROM GRACE

POEMS
BY
STEWART FLORSHEIM

BLUE LIGHT PRESS ◈ 1ST WORLD LIBRARY

1st WORLD
LIBRARY
Literary Society

AUSTIN ◈ FAIRFIELD ◈ DELHI

WINNER OF THE 2005 BLUE LIGHT BOOK AWARD

THE SHORT FALL FROM GRACE

1ST WORLD LIBRARY
PO Box 2211, Fairfield, Iowa 52556
www.1stworldlibrary.com

BLUE LIGHT PRESS
PO Box 642, Fairfield, Iowa 52556

COVER AND BOOK DESIGN:
By Melanie Gendron

COVER ART:
Man Writing in Artist's Studio
        by Gerard Dou, 1628-1631

AUTHOR PHOTO:
By Leon Borensztein

FIRST EDITION

LIBRARY OF CONGRESS CONTROL NUMBER:
2006900689

ISBN: 1595409823

ACKNOWLEDGMENTS

The following poems appeared in *Round Table*, 1986: "The Girl Eating Oysters," "The Jewish Singles Event," "The Best Bread in Montparnasse"

"The Jewish Singles Event" appeared in *Ghosts of the Holocaust* (Wayne State University Press, 1989) and in *Unsettling America: Race and Ethnicity in Contemporary American Poetry* (Viking Penguin, 1994)

"The *Kitchen Sink*" appeared in *Karamu*, 1993 (under the title, "The Hotel Albert, 1969") and in *Slipstream 19*, 1999

"My Father's Autopsy" appeared in *DoubleTake,* 2:4, Fall, 1996

"Recent Findings, 1996" appeared in *And What Rough Beast: Poems at the End of the Century* (under the title, "Recent Findings") (The Ashland Poetry Press, 1999)

"The Only Jew in Oswiecim" appeared in *Poetry on the Akeda as Modern Midrash* by Rabbi Steven Chester, 1999

"Exposed" appeared in *Rattle 14*, 2000

"Thirst" appeared in *88, A Journal of Contemporary American Poetry*, Issue 1, December, 2001 and *Compassion and Choices Magazine*, Volume 4, Number 1, Spring, 2005

"Survival" appeared in *the Seatttle Review* Volume XXV, Number 1, 2002

"Retribution" appeared in *Poetica*, 2003

"Initiation" and "The Unseen" appeared in *Full Circle*, Volume 1, Issue 6, 2003

"Mr. S" and "Once, After Swimming" appeared in *The 2River View*, Winter 8.2, 2004

The following poems appeared in Stewart Florsheim's chapbook, *The Girl Eating Oysters* (2River, 2004): "Mother to Son," "The Elevator," "Initiation," "The Cub Scout," "Parting Words," "The Girl Eating Oysters," "The Psychiatrist," "Munch, on Dagny Juell," "The Jewish Bride," "My Five-Year-Old Poses the Questions about God," "Survival," "Man on the Bus Gazes at this Roses," "Exposed," "My Father's Autopsy," "The Diagnosis," "The Hairdresser," "Thirst," "The Unseen," "Forsaken," "Unspoken"

"The Hairdresser" appeared in *The Great American Poetry Show, Volume 1* (The Muse Media, 2004)

"Munch, on Dagny Juell" and "Rembrandt, Petulant" appeared on *MesART.com*, January, 2005

Sincere thanks to the people who helped critique the work in this collection, including Thomas Centolella, Elizabeth Hope, Scott Norton, Evelyn Posamentier, and Elizabeth Rosner. And my deep appreciation to my wife Judy Rosloff and my daughters, Orli and Maya, for their love, support, and inspiration.

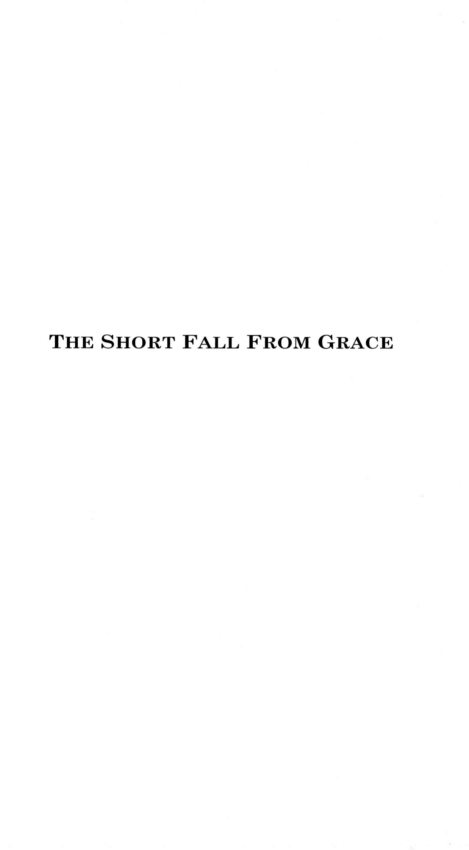

THE SHORT FALL FROM GRACE

In Memory of My Parents

If the earthly has forgotten
you, say to the still earth: I flow.
To the rushing water speak: I am.

from "Sonnet 29,"
The Sonnets to Orpheus: Second Series
by Rainer Maria Rilke
(as translated from the German by A. Poulin, Jr.)

TABLE OF CONTENTS

3.

4.

5.

MAN WRITING IN ARTIST'S STUDIO

after the painting, *Man Writing in Artist's Studio*
by Gerard Dou, 1628-1631

He doesn't know how to paint
so he makes the most of his words.
He sits in front of the easel
as the light streams in from the window behind.
He is careful as he forms each letter,
the letters becoming parts of words,
then parts of a journal entry, or a poem.
The painting has inspired him
perhaps in ways the artist never intended:
the expression on the mother's face
as she clings to her son
reminds him of his own mother,
the way she wanted him so much
he wasn't sure where his life began
and hers ended. His words seem to flow
from the painting, almost continuing it,
how his mother may have been affected
by the war, the shortage of food,
the inadequacies she found in her husband.
He was a good man, but hadn't she married
beneath herself, her parents constantly reminding her
that she was getting old, far too old to be selective
so when the boy came, she wanted to protect him,
there was no way he would survive without her.
The man continues writing without looking up
to view the painting again,
the light now reflecting only on his words.

1

Mark the first page of the book with a red marker.
For, in the beginning, the wound is invisible.

From *The Book of Questions*, by Edmond Jabés
(as translated from the French by Rosemarie Waldrop)

EDITH, TYPING ON THE BALCONY

after a family photograph, Frankfurt, June, 1939

It is a Sunday afternoon, the dishes
have been put away and she allows herself this—
she pulls out the typewriter, swings open the door
and takes the machine onto the narrow balcony.
A few months ago this would have been unthinkable
but the streets are empty and today she feels strangely
optimistic, so she begins her letter to America:
Heute ist das Wetter bild schön.
She can hardly contain herself as she writes about
the cat, Moorle, that her cousin left behind,
how it follows her around all day long
and sits on her shoulder as she does the dishes.
And the piece of chocolate Herr Schmidt gave her,
who cares if he did it out of pity,
she can still feel it melting in her mouth.
She mentions her younger brother Paul
who has just come onto the balcony with his camera
and what is he thinking, snapping a picture of her,
Er is doch so blöd, but if it comes out she will send it
next time along with news that things are getting better.
After all, didn't their fathers defend Germany in WW I—
in fact, she will enclose a photo of them she just found
and don't they look so proud, standing there in their uniforms.
Yes, today she just knows that things will get better,
immer besser. Wir grüssen euch. Edith.

ONCE, AFTER SWIMMING

I was in a shower in the Buena Vista Hotel
standing under my father's penis,
the long flesh over another pouch of flesh
that was surrounded by hair,
the soap and hot water running onto me in rivulets.
It was so unlike my mother's body,
the one I knew better,
the one that released me
only because it was my time.
She used to take me into her bath
while the tub was still filling
and the warm water enveloped us,
sealing off the rest of the world.

FIVE YEARS OLD

A day after I have my tonsils out
I decide I have had enough of the hospital
even though I love
the vanilla chocolate strawberry
ice-cream bars I get after lunch and dinner
so I get dressed,
take the elevator to the lobby
and start to leave
through the revolving door
although I have no clue
where I will go,
and then my mother enters
through the same revolving door
and I think it is the funniest thing
so we keep on going around and around
until I see my mother yelling at me,
she might even be crying,
her face is bright red
and then I can begin to hear her words:
Don't you ever do this to me again.

MOTHER TO SON

On Kristallnacht,
your grandfather had his bag packed
and was ready to go.
The Gestapo beat me up too
but back then they left little girls
with their mothers.
>   *Hoppe hoppe Reiter*
>   *Wenn er fällt dann schreit er*

Mr. Woolf, the man down the street
who lost his leg defending W.W. I Germany,
never imagined he would be taken.
Der Dank des Vaterlands ist euch gewiss, they said.
>   *Fällt er in den Graben*
>   *Fressen ihn die Raben*

Six weeks after they took your grandfather
I jumped up once at 2 AM. I knew
he was coming home. I ran outside,
down the street and there he was,
crying, crying, he cried for weeks.
>   *Fällt er in den Sumpf*
>   *Da macht er einen Plumps*

And then what happened
I keep asking, pushing through
one dark velvet curtain after another.

THE ELEVATOR

The man's pace quickens as he approaches me
in the lobby of our apartment building
next to the Port Authority,
the entry with the fake marble walls,
floor tiles in the shape of tiny diamonds
and the small elevator that creaks up
the six floors where everyone feels safe,
refugees from Dachau and Auschwitz,
the neighbors my mother invites over
to see my naked seven-year-old body,
comparing me to someone just out of the camps.
My genitals shrink as the man holds onto them, smiling,
I live on the sixth floor and my apartment is filled with candy,
the slits of his eyes open no wider than a knife blade.
You don't live here, I say, *I know everyone in the building,*
and then his grip tightens as he pulls me toward the elevator,
the one he wants to use to lift us above my village,
above the morass of the city—
the teenage boys who punched me in the face on 180th Street
or the ones who stole my UNICEF box on Halloween.
The man trembles now as he mentions the roof
where we can watch people get on and off buses
from cities like Englewood and Tenafly,
the rich people, unlike the two of us.
And as the light descends slowly down the shaft
I pray that the elevator is not empty
so when he pulls open the door
and Mrs. Duddel shuffles out demanding
in her wonderful Hungarian accent,*Where is your mother,*
I promise God I will not be angry with mom
for being late again as the man rushes out
into the heart of the city beating wildly
along with the souls of frightened little boys.

INITIATION

With my father in his meat locker—
the sides of large animals
hanging from their muscles,
the sinews that define the red meat
articulating former strength.
My father gives me a tour:
This is the piece that will become the filet.
This, we will sell as sirloin.
The sides swing around
as my father knocks into them,
unaware as they hit me when they swing back,
a nine-year-old tagging close behind,
hands covered in grease and blood.

MARTIN

It was too tempting not to press the 'B' button,
to listen to the elevator whir as it lowered me
into the bowels of the building where I might find
cockroaches and rats, walk the damp, dark corridor
to Martin's room, cracked green door, single cot
and Martin, smiling at the ten-year-old who defied
everyone in the building: *Don't go down there.*
But Martin with his gray felt hat, all he could do was smile,
scrub the floors and windows, help the old women
carry their groceries, change the occasional light bulb.
Our super said he saved him from a worse fate when they fled
Czechoslavakia but I stopped thinking of the super as a saint
the first time I saw him drunk, screaming so loudly at Martin
that the glass doors in our lobby rattled, Martin moped
and went down to his room where he would stay for days,
only the super's wife would go down with plates of boiled beef
and potatoes, and I would go down, sometimes with cookies.
It was during one of these exiles that Martin died.
Months later I would still go down to his room,
sit in the same chair I used to sit in when we would just
stare at each other and smile, I might talk
and Martin might try to mumble a few words in Czech
and I can still see him stand up, walk over to his picture of Prague
and point to the one building where he might have been born
or had a girlfriend and where I was sure,
at that moment, he was resting peacefully, away from
the super and his wife, mop and pail, the odor of ammonia
that followed him through the halls of our building.

THE CUB SCOUT

All my friends are moving up to Boy Scouts
but my mother doesn't think I'll make it
and how could I anyway with a father like mine,
As dumb as they come, he can't even spell the word camping.
She challenges him to teach me the basic knots
so we study the illustrations in the handbook
nights after he gets home from the butcher shop,
those big hands that cut up sides of beef
unsure whether the rope goes over or under the loop.
At the scoutmaster's we sit around
his formica kitchen table, the fluorescent light
flickering, and I can see my father
begin to sweat as the man pulls out the small rope,
my father already thinking of the words he will use
to haggle with the man when I can't tie the knots,
the way he haggles with customers who complain
the meat is too expensive, or he put his finger
on the scale while weighing the pastrami.
When we get home my mother is waiting at the front door
and I think now how I was conditioned to be loved too much
by women with as much self-contempt as she had.

SHIT. SHOWER. SHAVE.

Going to work for a day with my father
I am in a car with some of the other butchers,
the smell of blood cloying.
They talk about their wake-up rituals—
cursing the alarm as it ends an erotic dream,
acknowledging their morning boners
without time to wake up the missis
and then one of them chimes in,
Shit. Shower. Shave. I got it down.
It seems so reasonable that everyone becomes quiet
and when we get home my father mentions it again
either by way of advice or perhaps
he is impressed by the man's regularity
or the way the words sound,
my father's routine void of alliteration:
up at 5 AM, cautious not to wake my mother
and anxious to get out of the house,
even if his other life is a small butcher shop
in Spanish Harlem, a meat locker where the sides
of beef and pork spin alongside salami and head cheese,
tongues are stacked neatly in the back just below the shelf
where he keeps the kidneys, the testicles, the hearts.

MY FATHER'S CUE

Every so often my mother would laugh.
Mostly it was a joke about sex
and the laughter would begin deep
in her belly and continue for a minute or so
when she would say, *That was a good one.*
My father was always baffled.
Maybe it was her reaction to the subject
or the sound of the laughter—
my mother usually lashing out
at my father or sister, *his side of the family;*
my father, silent, thinking about the business,
better ways, perhaps, to display his cold cuts.
Even if others were around
he would tell my mother to keep laughing,
Before the evening is over, you'll be in tears.

MR. S

I can still feel him sidling into my wooden seat
carefully to avoid the creaking
while the rest of the class is at work
but all of us know our tenth-grade math teacher
does this with most of the boys.
He puts one arm around my shoulder and then
with the other he holds my pencil with me,
scratching out the algebra as though this is
the most natural thing to do, our hands
gliding across the page so that even writing X's and Y's
feels like one fluid motion. He stops
for a moment after writing the equal sign and
if I hesitate, he takes the lead,
his round face turning into a smile:
It is as simple as that.

THE *KITCHEN SINK*

It's Friday night so Ed, Gayle, and I
drive to Jahn's Ice Cream Parlor in The Bronx.
It's our high school haunt,
home of the *Kitchen Sink* that costs $6.95,
has at least twenty scoops of ice cream
or everything, the menu says, except the kitchen sink.
We meet four uniformed girls from Mother Cabrini High.
Mary tells us how much they hate their school—
no men, drugs, politics.
We tell them about George Washington High—
the muggings, students shooting up in the bleachers.
Our stories get us an invitation
to their party the next weekend:
They will rent a room in the Hotel Albert
and promise a wild time.

Room 24 is dark, only beds, bodies, smoke—
cigarettes, hash. The four girls
sit on a bed in their underclothes and in the center,
a man wearing only his jeans. Mary smiles,
This is Bill. We met him on the street this morning.
He's our hero. Then, moments later,
He did it to all of us, isn't that great?
We're all deflowered now.

Deflower: something to hang onto—
the Middle Ages, knights returning from battle
with stories about the lands they conquered,
women they raped. But no, this is 1969, Greenwich Village
and these are girls from parochial school
boasting about *their* achievements.
And Gayle — who still can't decide if Ed or I
should be the first one, our condoms

16

making indelible marks on our wallets.
Bill doesn't say a word, no one does,
until Simon and Garfunkel come on the AM radio
and everyone joins them:
Sail on silvergirl, sail on by.
Your time has come to shine.
All your dreams are on their way.

PARTING WORDS

Before I go off to college
my father gives me the only advice he ever will:
Don't get venereal disease.
We are standing near the front door
of the apartment, my cartons packed—
books, journals, clothing, records,
the stereo that folded neatly into a box.
My father had never spoken to me about sex before,
he had never spoken to me much at all,
my mother always managing to prevent that:
You can't talk to him, what does he know anyway?
Farmers. His father had a cattle ranch in Hünfeld.
She would always emphasize the umlauted 'u'
to make sure we heard the reference to "chicken."
But that comment always drew me closer to him,
a farm life to a boy growing up in New York City—
my father getting up just before sunrise
to milk the cows or go to cattle auctions with his dad.
My father and I are standing face-to-face now,
eighteen years of being in the same apartment,
my mother and sister fighting day and night,
the screaming, slamming doors, slaps across the face:
Don't get venereal disease.

When I was a boy I heard loud noises on the other side
of the same front door where we are standing now
so I opened the tiny metal blinds that covered the peephole.
A teenage girl was outside wielding a knife
and when she saw my eye, she lunged for it.

RECENT FINDINGS, 1996

The ingots of gold, they say,
were once the fillings of Jews' teeth
and now the bars are in vaults in Zurich
and New York, in the Federal Reserve Bank
where my mother landed a job as a messenger
and her bosses calculated the Swiss debt
against the gold that might have belonged
to her aunts or uncles, the gold they used
to chew their boiled beef and potatoes
during family gatherings on Sunday afternoons
where the topic of conversation would be
how quickly all of this madness will pass.

RETRIBUTION

On a return trip to Frankfurt sponsored by German government
the clerk at the Frankfurter Hof wants to put my mother
into a room the size of a small closet.
She goes back to the front desk shaking her passport in his face:
You invited us back to ask our forgiveness.
He offers excuses—a bankers' convention,
the busloads of tourists from Bulgaria.
She turns around and there they are tugging
big brown suitcases through revolving doors.
But my mother does not budge, eats two of the welcome apples,
frowns at the clerk strutting his high German,
wonders what his grandfather did during the war.
The clerk tries to ignore her so the passport takes on a life
of its own as my mother starts shaking it
in front of the concierge, the manager, the tourists from Bulgaria.

She gets escorted to the luxury suite
that has two rooms with views of the city,
a telephone in the bathroom. She calls me in California:
They can't push me around anymore.

DECEMBER, 1999

In the newspaper, the faces of remorse:
A congressman running for office
says the US should have tried to stop
the killing of millions in Rwanda—
next to him, photos of a mass grave,
the girl with a swollen stomach.
A German manufacturer comes up
with another billion marks for slave laborers.
When I was a boy I was so skinny
my mother used to parade my naked body
in front of the neighbors who also were survivors—
See, doesn't he look like he just came out of Dachau?
I imagined I might still be alive in the year 2000
and how carefully I did the math:
carrying the ones
as though they were made of crystal.

A man may lose his head, yet come to no harm.

St. Thomas More

MIDNIGHT COWBOY

Eight of us men pile into Paul's '68 Chevy.
It's freezing cold, snowing, but we can't take it anymore
in the dorm, or in college, or in upstate New York.
It's just before finals and we're freaking out,
the long No-Doz nights, the amphetamines
before the double whammy, two finals in one day,
Existentialism, and Journalism and The Law.
We drive down Erie Boulevard past Abe's Donuts,
stop in a local deli for two six-packs
then head to a drive-in to see *Midnight Cowboy*.
Some of us have seen the movie and imitate Voight
as he approaches a woman on Park Avenue:
Ma'am, can you tell me where the Statue of Liberty is?

Ken can't wait to see Voight's sexual feats again,
describing them in such detail the car fogs up
and Paul tells him to shut up till the defroster gets going.
Then Ken tells us about a double X-rated film he saw:
I got so horny I started to play with myself
but the movie finished before I did.

We get to the drive-in and the cashier tells us we're welcome
but the car heaters that are left are all broken.
We consider going in anyway, it's only ten below zero
and we have the beer, the heat generated by eight of us
who are by now horny, rowdy and possessed by a grace
that will allow us to survive anything at all.

SWEET REVENGE

Freshman year in college, finals week, I have 103,
mono, and this is the time my roommate chooses
to get even with me for not being gay.
He invites the man into our room, smell of beer
now mingling with the bag of vomit near my head.
I hear the LP drop on my stereo—
Ravel, by the Vienna Philharmonic—
and Ron's whispers, *Oh, just ignore him.*
I open my eyes to see them dancing and necking,
then the rattle of buckles and rustle of clothing,
the slurps and moans, first of one person, then two.
I am back in high school, Gayle's bedroom,
our tongues twining as a glob of red lava ascends
to the top of the lamp inches from the bed.
Gayle is not sure we should be doing this
but still she is urging me on,
the *Bolero* now reaching its height.

THE GIRL EATING OYSTERS

after the painting, *The Girl Eating Oysters*
by Jan Steen, 1658-1660

It is not this moment that matters:
the girl looking up suddenly
as she sprinkles pepper on an oyster
in the backroom of the oyster shop.
Her eyes say that she deserves this fare—
the oysters, already opened
lying neatly on the tablecloth,
the bread and screw of pepper
on a silver platter,
a glass of white wine.
In a second she will begin her feast
and already her body is tingling
even before she takes
the first oyster in her mouth.
And as she takes the first
she will anticipate the second,
then the third.
She will eat the last oysters quickly
then rush out through the oyster shop
looking both ways before she leaves.
She will run down the cobblestone street,
up the narrow flight of stairs
and, ever so slowly, open
her lover's front door.

LONGING

On a train from Mashad to Teheran,
making love to a woman who came to meet me
from Amsterdam. She told me she loved me
and I could only murmur a few words
that would get confused with the screeching and
clanging, the incessant stops in towns like
Sabzevor, Shahrud, Semnan. Somehow
we had made it through Afghanistan,
summer heat, old school buses breaking down
in the desert. They were filled with sheep
and large men wearing white djellabahs
and foreigners, their eyes yellow and tired.
Once we got to Herat at 4 AM we couldn't
get into the city because the guards were asleep
so we rested alongside the bus. We fantasized
about Persia, the mosques of Isfahan
as we watched the sun rise over the minarets
and listened to the muezzin begin their call:
they were wailing and it sounded like song.

CAPRICE

Frau Gräfin, das Souper ist serviert.
—from the opera, *Capriccio*, by Richard Strauss

The Countess Madeleine has not yet chosen
the man she will marry, she must know
in just a few hours, and already the Major-Domo
wants to serve her supper: medallions of venison,
fresh spätzle, Porcini mushrooms, Schwarzwurzel.
She thinks this is all preposterous,
the dinner (and now the urn of Liebfraumilch),
the fact that she must even choose between two men,
the composer or the poet. And to think,
with her crystalline-blue eyes and blond hair,
the family money, she was sure she would be swept
off her feet. Her father would call her his *Schätzchen*
as did his friends, who would laugh
as they tried to touch her in all the wrong places.
She opens the two large windows in the drawing room,
closes her eyes and hears Mozart's *Ch'io mi scordi*,
his lilting rhythms make her sway.
But suddenly she is troubled by the absence
of words, she needs them to help her define
this moment: the moon, so full and so near, the stars
in complicity with everything that is dark around her.

THE SCHEME

after the painting, *Curiosity*
by Gerard ter Borch, 1660

The woman is writing a letter to her suitor
and although she knows her sister is standing
over her shoulder reading each word
she proceeds to tell him about another man
who is pursuing her, a man from a better family
that has been in the Draper's Guild for years.
She knows her sister will tell her best friend
who will no doubt tell her father who will
in turn tell the innkeeper, so her suitor will find out
even before he gets the letter.
And though the other man doesn't exist,
the woman can already imagine her suitor
dashing into their foyer and getting on his knees
and then she will break the news to her parents
who will throw a lavish party on the Herengracht,
the chandeliers so polished she will look up
and see her smile on hundreds of crystal drops.

RENDEZVOUS, CASABLANCA

Nine PM at the airport in Casablanca.
My plane gets in first
then it seems as though every plane
is arriving at once except hers—
Swissair, Air France, British Airways,
then finally Alitalia. We embrace
in what seems like the center of the world
then the hours to clear customs.
The drunk man from England who was on my plane
is standing in front of us. He insists
we follow a certain route with him—
to head south immediately into the desert
so we stay clear of all tourists,
the bane of Morocco.
As he pulls the map out of his pack
the authorities notice his open Scotch:
Please sirs, it's Christmas. I'm travelling alone
and this is a gift I bought for myself.

On the other side of the double-glass doors
we check through our copy of Frommer's
then head for the Hotel Guylemer.
All through the night and day the hall toilet
gurgles like a powerful but distant river
and then the dreams: the turbulent ocean,
the whale that gets washed ashore
and picked apart by penguins then becomes
a horse that gallops into the water. Our bodies
roll into each other on the straw mattress
and we wake up. Strong and furious it is
like riding a beast that cannot be broken.

THE TURKISH BATHS, FEZ

The baths, they tell me, are difficult to find:
Go up rue d'Espagne, left at the top of the hill,
down a long, winding road
(toujours, la droite; toujours, la droite)
then right before rue Slimane that has no street sign.
Inside, the words are peeling from the walls—
SEULEMENT LES HOMMES—
and the men are there, families it seems,
each one lined up for a ticket and towel.

In the steamy room I take my place,
my small towel around me, a fig leaf.
Still everything remains hidden—
a gutter of water borders the room
and men sit along it alone,
their legs stretched across, a mountain stream.
Some recite from the Koran, other sit silently,
thoughts drifting away from the souks—
the peppery smells of cumin and smen,
mounds of couscous and rows of khelea,
yelling merchants, screaming babies.

An old man appears with a bucket of soapy water.
He sits behind me and without a word
scrubs my back, then chest, legs.
His sweat drips onto my body along with
condensation from the cracked ceiling.
He gives me a massage and I know
he has been doing this for years, his hands drawn
to the tension in my neck. Before he moves
to the next man I want to praise him
but know the words would begin
the short fall from grace.

MEDINA

Walking through the medina in Fez you ask me
if any two people could ever be as close as we are,
a question as simple as the young man asking for a *baksheesh*,
his eyes squinting in the sun as he looks at us
and then we look at each other, embarrassed,
not by the man, the same one who tried to rip us off
days before in the shop full of lapis lazuli,
but by our naivete, how easy it seems to go
from having so much to having so little.
We spend the rest of the day very near each other,
drinking mint tea in stalls full of brass, carpets,
their designs no less intricate than the medina itself
where we walk, arms hooked into each other,
talking only about the things that grab our senses:
there, the sulfurous smell from the tannery,
a wall covered with purple and green leather hides,
the voice of the muezzin calling the faithful to prayer.

THE PSYCHIATRIST

He sways through the room like a peacock,
opens his feathers, then sits down.
It's his power strut, the one
disguised as beauty and sensitivity:
he wants to hear my dreams.
I read them from my journal
and he doesn't say a word until I finish,
a whole week of the unconscious,
You're doing much better.
He struts to his desk for a phone call
and returns. *Where were we?*
Your dream about Tunisia...
No, I say, *Morocco.* He cocks his head,
offers a few words—anima, mother complex.
He wants to know why I don't settle down,
says he hates to travel, even hates to drive,
makes him nervous. He rests his bird legs
on the ottoman and studies me and I am gone,
into the labyrinth of the medina in Meknes,
around one corner and then the next.
The rain beats down and not one thought
about ever finding my way out.

MUNCH, ON DAGNY JUELL

after the lithograph, *Jealousy II*
by Edvard Munch, 1896

Everything about her is irresistible:
her long black hair that falls into my face
when we make love,
her red lips the color of blood flower.
And what's more, she loves me too
even though she is the wife of my close friend
and risks her marriage to meet me afternoons
in my studio in the backstreets of Berlin.
Her husband is outraged but she claims
he does not know her as well as I do
or the other men at the *Café zum schwarzen Ferkel*.
Yes, she has been with a few of them too
but she says I am her most passionate lover,
when I gaze into her eyes I see her soul
and there is nothing she can hide.
In truth, she says, I can never belong to any man,
I am too weak, and then she says,
we are too weak, Edvard, that is why
we will never stay together
and why we need each other so much
we embrace like this in the afternoon light—
surely all of Berlin can see.

ON THE PALISADES

Mendocino: morning air wet
like the eyes of the woman
alone on the beach.
The man climbs the high cliffs,
his feet curling round edges.
He wants to be near her
but he knows this desire —
it is not for the woman,
no, not for her,
but for something about her:
the way both of them love the sea,
the insistence of the waves,
the fog lifting, always lifting.

The woman is below him now.
She looks up and calls him again
and again. He looks down, trembling,
remembering the night before
when they were making love
and she screamed his name
and he pushed and pushed for her
as hard as he could.

THE BEST BREAD IN MONTPARNASSE

after the painting, *Le Dejeuner Sur L'Herbe*
by Edouard Manet, 1863

Perhaps she is only a thought:
the man in the black hat
talks about a woman he made love to once
in the Bois de Boulogne
and his friend conjures up her image—
naked, red hair tied back, innocent.

He imagines what she looks like making love,
her eyes half shut, half focused
on her other life:
the long walk alone to her flat
where her husband waits for her,
his disinterest so strong
he drops his Pernod as she walks in.
Or maybe he is with his mistress and the flat is empty,
not quite as cold as if he were in his study
and she lights a fire, pulls out her Flaubert.

The man in the black hat offers
his friend a bunch of grapes and he snaps back
into the conversation: the Impressionist show at the Salon,
the new café on the Blvd. St. Germain.

In the back of his mind he has decided
that tonight he will visit his mistress
and although she is not well-read
she bakes the best bread in Montparnasse.
And when he comes over she will know
to put the bread in the oven and watch it rise,
slowly, as he talks about his morning in the café
on the Rue St. Lazare, the afternoon in the park
with his friend from the south.

ON A LETTER TO MILENA

> In spite of everything, writing does one good. I'm calmer than
> I was two hours ago with your letter outside on the deck chair.
> Kafka to Milena, 1920

As though her letter said something about the shyness
of their correspondence or merely
the tulips, opening yesterday, reminded her
of a train ride she took to Marienbad as a girl.
There is no doubt she said something
that affected him and he wanted to please her
with his response. He wanted to say
the right thing without sounding patronizing
even though he knew she would forgive him.
He begins: *Dear Frau Milena....About some letters*
you complain that you turn them in all directions
and nothing falls out of them, and yet they are,
if I'm not mistaken, just those in which I feel
so close to you, so tamed in my blood and taming yours,
that one doesn't really want to say anything
but that up there, through the trees
the sky is visible, that's all....

He finishes the letter, folds into it
rows and rows of fir trees, a small patch of sky
and he wonders if she can see it as well,
he will ask her in tomorrow's letter if she can see it:
the clearing through the trees,
the bright, bright blue.

INTO FLIGHT

after the painting, *Eleven AM*
by Edward Hopper, 1926

The woman seems oblivious to the fact
that she is naked, sitting in front
of a large open window of a city building.
Perhaps it is because she is already wearing
her shoes, the navy blue ones with the flat heels,
and just got distracted while dressing,
the outfit she chose lying neatly on her bed
(the red dress, blue sweater, gold chain).
It could have been the way the light
was falling into the room in slanted sheets
or her lover's idle chatter during breakfast,
how it betrays his decision. It could have been
a falcon making its nest between concrete blocks—
the way it soars around tall buildings
always returning with home in its beak:
there, a few leaves, twigs, pieces of string.
In a couple of moments she will stand up,
stretch, and imagine what it would feel like
to take those few steps into flight—
not unlike a falcon, gracing the city.

SINCE WE PARTED

In a pensione room
on a quiet street in Rome
the sun enters
through the shutters.
First it reaches the sink,
the marble counter,
then the old oak armoire.
It crosses the yellow tile floor
then covers the bed, once warm,
now brilliant with light.

Cleansed even of our appetite for bliss,
we'd only want to know the ground of our new wonder,
and we wouldn't be surprised to find that
it survived where we'd known it had all along,
in all for which we'd blamed ourselves, repented
and corrected, and never for a moment understood.

From *The Knot,* by C.K. Williams

THE WOMAN IN FIESOLE

after the painting, *Afternoon in Fiesole*
by Baccio Maria Bacci, 1926-1929

The woman is unmistakably sad
as she listens to her friend's husband
play the guitar on a Sunday afternoon,
a song the grape pickers sing during the harvest.
She remembers a happier time ten years before
when she worked in the vineyards with her lover.
They were drunk then on everything but the wine—
the bright golds of Tuscany,
the promises they would make to each other
for the perfect life.

In a moment she will walk away from the window
and take a fig from the table.
The texture will take her back,
her tongue discovering the inside
of her lover's mouth,
the words they would offer each other:
love, freedom, solitude.
She will look out over Fiesole
shivering in the afternoon light.

THE JEWISH SINGLES EVENT

Here are those who are challenged by
It's hard to meet someone,
those who have taken to heart
not only the importance of marriage
but marriage to the right person.
We surround the dance floor and
just like in summer camp,
the men are on one side, women on the other.
The band begins with a tune by the Stones.
A bold man, the one with the beard
and the Calvin Klein suit who has no doubt
considered law school, medical school
and is now a photographer,
walks over to the woman in gold lamé shoes.
She seems so disinterested that
an earthquake would not startle her,
the chandelier, falling from the ceiling,
would seem like an ocean of diamonds.

Moms and dads of the world, look how hard we are trying.
Wasn't it easier forty years ago when marriages
were arranged and survival was the issue.
You had watched lovers holding each other
through barbed wire fences
and had heard about the experiments on the wombs
of Jewish women. You wanted us to have a better life
so you have given us everything you could not have—
the finest clothing, appliances that can
spin, blend, chop, dice the most wilted produce.
And a world where we can choose what we want to do
and whether or not we want to marry.
We haven't come a long way to want to live alone,
but it is easy. Only the ghosts are there:
their branded arms embrace us.

THE JEWISH BRIDE

after the painting, *The Jewish Bride*
by Rembrandt, 1667

The man's hands resolve into hers
as though this union started years before they meet
at the synagogue on the Judenbreestraat.
She is sixteen, he nineteen and his family
with the shipbuilding business in Rotterdam.
The marriage seems destined, the parents amazed
a Jewish couple can meet and fall in love
without an arrangement. Once the marriage
is announced, plans are made that will take years
to complete—the engagement party, wedding,
the new house on the Prinsengracht,
the portrait that can only be done by Rembrandt.
On the way to his studio they have their first argument—
his plans to go hunting twice a year with his friends
from the Gymnasium, boys she doesn't like in the least
but even if she did she wants to be asked beforehand—
so when Rembrandt poses them the woman wonders
if she made a mistake, and the painter
captures that moment, the woman looking away
from her fiancé, unsure whether catching his gaze
she will call off all plans, or become the wife
who will forever be waiting for her husband to return.

MARY POPPINS

When we pack up the goldfish
in the Double Rainbow ice-cream container
to take it to my daughter's new preschool
I tell her how happy it will be
in the larger tank with the other goldfish
and because she is not quite sure
she wants to carry the fish,
she will not let go of it for a second
even as I buckle her into her car seat,
and as soon as we get to school
we empty the fish into the tank,
the three-year-old noses pressed against it,
and she says, *Look, there's Mary Poppins,*
and they are amazed watching the fish
swim freely in its new world.

MY FIVE-YEAR-OLD POSES THE QUESTION ABOUT GOD

The beauty is it comes up as easily
as the fight she had with Lauren at school
because Lauren told her she wouldn't be her best friend
anymore if she did not share her fruit roll-up.
My daughter wonders if God will think she is bad
and then, what does He look like anyway. Is He,
in fact, a He or a She, black or white.
She asks if God is the echo she hears
when she makes loud noises in tunnels
and if He is the wind that makes kites
climb way up to the sky. What amazes me most
is the assumption that God exists and I hesitate
when I tell her that some people don't believe in God
and some people believe in many gods.
Some people even think monkeys are gods.
She is quiet for a moment and then,
pointing to the fat little monarch on top of
King's Auto Repair, *That's Him.*
I know for sure. That's Him.

RAPPEL

At the City Rock my six-year-old is learning
how to climb cliffs. She puts on her harness,
I snap the photo and she ascends
a 30-foot wall with handles and crevices.
Halfway up she stops, looks down at me
and I yell up, *Go ahead, you can do it*,
watching my own six-year-old body, breathless,
so frail my parents have to feed me
eggs in chocolate milk, *the real egg cream*,
they laugh, baffled because I had stopped eating.
My daughter looks up again,
continues to climb. I can feel the strain
in her thin arms, I can hear her body sigh
as she reaches the top then refuses
to budge. I yell up again, the instructor
has to climb up to coax her down and moments later
she rappels down the wall slowly, her legs
as short as mine were, each kick unsure,
scared, still unaccustomed to anger.

SURVIVAL

Sixth grade: my daughter wants me to test her
on Darwin's theory, how the only species
that survive are those that adapt
and we think about examples—
the birds that develop longer beaks
so they can pull their food out of the marsh,
humans and their ability to walk.
What I want is to tell her
the other face to survival:
How my grandfather had his bag packed
ready to go to Dachau on Kristallnacht
because he believed *das Vaterland*
would come through for him.
How my father started ignoring my mother
even as her screaming at him got louder and louder
until I had to ask him one day, how can he take it
and he had no idea what I was talking about.
How I stopped eating when I was five
and became too weak to walk up stairs.
Call it an urge to disappear:
the sky itself becoming so large it envelops us
and we let it, we give in, we do not fight.

REVERIE

During lunch at Hunan Home's,
scallops in black bean sauce,
sizzling rice that seems to quiet us,
you say, *We should have gotten married,*
words that fill us, then make us hungry,
not that we would have been good together
but for a few moments we share our longing,
the way the conductor walked up and down
the train this morning advising passengers
how to fulfill their goals and they listened,
or the way the big oak stood over Horse Mountain
and you used to run up to it to watch
the colts run by those winter afternoons.
Timing was against us, I say—
call it your anger after a failed marriage
or my fear that we were getting too close—
even as the horses walked by your window
and we listened to Chopin Sunday mornings
eating pancakes filled with blackberries from your garden.

HER OTHER LIFE

after the painting, *Woman Holding a Balance*
by Johannes Vermeer, 1662-1664

The woman is taking stock of her life,
her coins and jewels, the lover
she gave up when she found out
she is pregnant, hoping against hope
the child is her husband's.
After all, he is a good man even though
she never would have chosen him:
the prominent family with the house on the Herengracht,
the textile business worth millions
and her friends tell her he is handsome.
Besides, she knows he loves her
and he will be an excellent father,
the child will go to the best Gymnasium in Amsterdam.

She has a sad smile, the kind
that will always know the tragedy
of compromise. She was her father's favorite
and didn't he say she would have the best,
that no one would ever be good enough.
She will continue to think of her lover
when she makes love to her husband.
When he enters her, she will move
into her other life, that is the only moment
the four of them will be together,
when she can call out to her husband, her lover,
her child, *I want you inside of me. I am yours.*

MAN ON THE BUS GAZES AT HIS ROSES

He knows nothing about roses so he wonders
if he was taken: are they fragrant enough,
are the buds too opened or too closed,
are the stems the right length. He wonders
how hard he tries to please his wife
and even though it is their anniversary
he wonders if he tries too hard, shouldn't there be
more joy in their comings and goings,
the way the man across from him saved a seat
for his partner and now his arms are around her
as they joke and read from the same magazine.
When the man gets off the bus he holds the roses
carefully, almost too tightly, to his chest:
they have turned into crystal and look exquisite.

SAG PANEER

Eating dinner at an Indian restaurant
you tell me you haven't had sex
with your wife for years.
You look at me for a reaction
and I mumble words about
how we learn to live
with what we need most
but my mind is focused
on the sag paneer:
the white cheese rising to the top
of a green sea.

THE MESSENGER

after the painting, *The Messenger*
by Pieter de Hooch, 1670

Her husband has no doubt reached the East Indies again
and this is the letter she waits for, the one where he describes
the rambutan, snake fruit, durian,
the women with baskets on their heads
filled with orchids, bananas, chicken.
He usually says this is all they can do with their heads
but those words don't register, she even forgives
the guns and cannons, the machetes she hears about
from the green grocer. She knows the Dutch
will free the heathens, bring the right god.
She recognizes the stamps and opens the letter quickly,
The rambutan are sweeter than ever this year,
but then the tone changes, he has been thinking,
too much blood-letting, the people are quite civil
after all. She says to herself she understands
when he writes he won't be back for several years,
he will be teaching new ways of farming.
She won't consider that perhaps he has taken a lover
so she ponders his goodness, his desire to help,
the way he offers to water Mevrouw van Hall's geraniums
when she goes to Italy to take the baths.
The woman folds up the letter, walks out to her young daughter
who is just approaching the Keizersgracht with her fishing rod
and gives her a small hug, *Veel plezier, jonge.*
And then she smiles, *Dag, tot ziens*, to the messenger
who has already walked into the bakery down the street,
his eyes fixed on the eclairs just being moved into the showcase.

SAYING GRACE

Carving up the turkey
she seems almost magnanimous,
a surgeon performing without a fee.
When she severs the thigh from the leg
she makes it seem natural.
A woman like that would kill for her family.
Would you like dark meat or light?
The children always seem greedy.
The husband never says a word
even though he is always struck
by how beautiful she looks in red.

THE MARRIED

A coffee shop on San Pablo on a Friday night,
a man plays guitar, another plays bass.
The shop is empty but neither seems to care.
They are playing the blues, their faces contorting
around words like *love, loneliness*,
how a man can hold the face of his beloved
and still weep, and he wants to live
in that moment — its truth is blessed.
The musicians are oblivious
to the two people standing outside
in the falling rain,
their faces pressed against the glass.

GLI SPOSI

after the Etruscan sculpture, *Gli Sposi*, 3rd-2nd century BC

The old couple is finishing a meal,
she, lying alongside the banquet table,
he, at the head, and perhaps the husband
made a disparaging comment—something about
the way she trained the servants,
the hare once again underdone—and the wife
can only respond with the same look
she has given him for years.
For moments the rest of the world disappears
until a servant brings a bowl of fruit
and they attack it greedily then retreat,
each one contemplating a small bunch of grapes,
resplendent in the diminishing light.

FAITH

Perhaps Abraham was only striving for perfection.
Isaac would have burned, joy shooting from his fingertips.

On a billboard, *Leadership. Accountability. Vote Yes.*
Near a child's desk, a globe explodes and coins rain over the room.

Keith Jarrett on keyboards and the city sleeps,
ears and feet turned to the heavens.

The other wife, always lurking behind corners
while the children are in bed dreaming of ogres and heroines.

To the Jewish mystics, creation out of nothing means the same
          as creation out of God.
When an infant comes into the world, we tremble.

Open closed open. Before we are born, everything is open
in the universe without us. For as long as we live,
everything is closed
within us. And when we die, everything is open again.
Open closed open. That's all we are.

from *Open Closed Open*, by Yehuda Amichai
(as translated from the Hebrew by Chana Bloch and Chana Kronfeld)

AFTER THE EMERGENCY PHONE CALL

I take the red eye to New York,
my mother's words racing with the engine,
He's a religious man, maybe he'll pull through,
then to the tenth floor of the Milstein Pavilion
where I walk into the ICU smiling,
This is a surprise visit, a business trip,
offering him one of *their* lies,
my parents keeping everything from the children:
the way my grandfather was packed
ready to go to Dachau on Kristallnacht,
my grandmother's heart attack,
my mother's breast cancer.
Surely my father must know how sick he is—
the monitors strapped to his chest,
the catheter out of the helpless bud of his penis.
But he lifts his body, smiles,
wants to know where he is,
then tells me he's ready to go home now
and I say, no, they might operate tomorrow,
and he orients himself with the hope
like the times my mother finally left the refuge
of our small bathroom where she would sit for hours
after condemning my father and sister,
his side of the family. And even if he did know
he would never wake up from surgery,
he would still accept his death peacefully
so as not to make a fuss,
he would still ask my mother
if she had eaten his homemade meatloaf for dinner
then throw her a kiss through his oxygen mask.

MY FATHER'S AUTOPSY

The room is cold and bright,
so unlike our dark kitchen in Washington Heights
where he sat silently, oblivious
to my mother yelling about his inadequacies,
my sister chatting on her Princess phone.
When he finished his meal
he pushed his plate back across the table
next to mine, that is as close as we got,
his baked potato skins curling against my milk glass,
the fatty rind of his steak nuzzling my string beans.
The doctors don't notice his silence now.
For all they know, he was the model father
who spent quality time with the kids—
Shea Stadium, fishing trips, the walks
when he would dispel our fears about
Harvey, the bully next door, or Mrs. Kipperman,
the neighbor with the numbers branded on her arm.
The doctors are most interested in his brain,
perhaps they will unravel a passion we never knew—
a woman who walked into his meat market 25 years before,
an opera he heard when he was a young man in Germany.
Perhaps they will hold his brain to the light
and find the truth about his silence,
that somewhere along the way he got broken
and it hit him while ringing up
a pound of cold cuts, a pint of coleslaw
or when my mother called him an idiot
in front of my friends.
But the report tells me nothing:
Necrosis of cerebral cortex.
Loss of neurons in thalamus.
It says he became comatose during surgery
when his heart stopped for several minutes,
his words fluttering inside his chest:
the wings of a dying crow.

TO MY FATHER

I wanted to see you on your deathbed
because I prayed you would fight against your dying
so unlike the way you took a stand against anything—
your wife screaming that you are stupid
then explaining to me in the same loud voice,
Ach, I could have done much better,
there was that good-looking man,
then the optometrist, but she followed
her dad's advice, *Always the good girl.*

How I wanted you to tell the doctors to fuck off,
break away from the tubes and catheters
that were reaming every orifice,
then the two of us could have gone to Hünfeld,
you always wanted to do that,
recount the joys and fears through landmarks—
the farm on which you were born,
the park where your father beat you for stealing a toy,
the first place you had sex.

But perhaps that trip wasn't necessary,
your youth was a story, as simple and well-defined
as everything else in your life:
the job you got waiting on tables
the day after your boat arrived from Germany,
your meat market where I remember
the blood on the floor mixed with sawdust,
it smelled so much like the earth,
it was basic, like the fact of your dying
and that you would accept it quietly,
gracefully, my father who loved me
simply because I was his son.

PROPHECY

My mother calls to tell me she fell
as soon as she left the hairdresser's,
her forehead striking the pavement
and the throngs of New Yorkers who surround her
but only the few who offer support,
Someone went to call 911, honey, don't move.
She sees her blood dripping onto the sidewalk
and suddenly it all makes sense,
that familiar fear, only strangers
staring down at her, the lack of air.
Later in the ambulance she will recall
giving birth, how she lay in a room by herself
screaming, my head was crowning
and the nurse would come in every few minutes,
Keep your legs together for god's sake, the doctor is late.
But for now there are only voices—
Don't worry, the ambulance, blanket
in English, Spanish, Korean, Cantonese—
and somehow they calm her,
even the faint wail of the siren is comforting,
the cold sidewalk holding her cheek.

THE DIAGNOSIS

We do everything but name the disease.
My mother wants to know if it is curable
and the words begin to bounce off the walls:
nerves, muscles, breath, stop
muscles, nerves, stop, breath.
She knows this silence
so she just looks at me and will not let go.
Back on the street a sudden gale so strong
I can barely push my mother's wheelchair up the hill.
A tug-of-war, perhaps, in reverse
as I imagine trying to deliver my mother
but her wheelchair knocks me down and this time
there is nothing I can do to save her.

THE HONEYMOONERS

From my mother's bedroom
the sound of a TV clicked on.
It is 1AM and she no longer
wants to think about the disease.
She switches from one channel to the next
and stops at *The Honeymooners.*
Ralph is yelling at Alice
about spending a weekend in the Catskills:
Classes in ballroom dancing! Bridge!
He repeats the word *Bridge* for the benefit
of Norton who has no doubt
just walked in and slammed the door.
The canned laughs roll out of the bedroom
and fill the apartment.
The black and white light flickers in the corridor.
A mote of dust rises from the floor.

CLUES

Doing the Sunday *Times* crossword
after learning that she only has
a few months left to live.
My mother searches for clues:
Capital of Bhutan. Six letters.
Louvre pyramid designer.
Sappho's poet friend.

On a small pad on her night table
the words *Hemlock Society*
written in pencil,
the letters tiny, shaken.

FROMAGE

At 5 AM my mother wakes me
yelling in French: *Fromage. Fromage.*
She keeps pointing to her mouth
because it is getting hard to talk.
I bring her a piece of brie
but she shakes her head, no.
Juice. What is the word?
I bring orange juice with the usual dose
of morphine and she smiles.
She shuts her eyes and I imagine she is back
in Volksschule, learning French.
The class is still on the segment about meals—
Käse, fromage. Käse, fromage.
The teacher wants the class to repeat after her
and my mother, the perfect student,
is very clear: *Fromage. Fromage.*

THIRST

My mother and I are given careful instructions
on how to hasten her death.
Once you stop drinking, it's only a matter of days.
When I was a boy I was so frail
I could barely walk up a flight of stairs.
Dr. Turnauer told my mother to force me to eat:
Try anything. Raw egg yolks in chocolate milk.
I can still see my mother separating the yolk
from the egg white until she only had the yellow center
back in its cracked shell,
the albumen dripping reluctantly into the porcelain sink.
She would drop the yolk into the dark brown liquid
and beat it as hard as she could,
then hold up the container to see if the yolk had disappeared
but it was elusive, the light always detecting
the yellowish wisps that would help me survive.

PASSAGE

After spending a year
coming to terms with the disease
my mother looks at me
and says *I'm sorry.*
Already her body barely
leaves an impression
on the jelly pad the hospice brought in
to prevent bedsores.
Her watch slides off her wrist
and lands quietly on the quilt,
then disappears in the down.
The unread *New York Times* are piled
on my father's side of the bed,
each issue opened to the crossword,
the unfilled boxes no longer
ask for a clue.

THE FINISH

On a TV drama a husband and wife are fighting
and my mother wants me to help them.
I tell her no, this is TV, there is nothing I can do
but she doesn't understand.
Go help them. Please,
as though we were still living in the old apartment,
my mother yelling at my father again
because he brought home the wrong coffee
or why can't he play poker like the other men,
and my father in one of his rare moments
starts screaming at her
and I want her plastered to the wall, this time
I am with him all the way.

THE HAIRDRESSER

When my mother becomes ill the hairdresser
she has known for the past 30 years—
the only one who can fix my hair the way I like—
comes to her apartment. He is always drunk
and calls her by a different name—
their own inside joke. She would laugh
but by the end she didn't respond,
assuming that she may well be Mrs. Kaufman
or one of the other names he called out.
When he washed her hair I could see
she was all forehead, the few strands he teased
over the front giving her a face.
Just before she died my mother's eyes
could only reach the bottom of the mirror
but she would still try to hand him the rollers
and stare while he placed the thin strands around each one
as though he alone could tether her to this earth.

RAGGEDY ANN

Finding my mother in bed,
mouth still opened around a last breath
after we looked into all the ways
she could hasten the end,
stop the disease that was making her body
as flaccid as a Raggedy Ann.
She used to love that doll and
picking it up off my daughter's bed
she would hug it tightly and joke with her:
Can I borrow the doll, just for tonight?
I want to hug her to death all night long.

THE BODY

My mother's hair looks fine
(she would have been pleased)
the setting still in place, encircling her head.
Gone the voice that pleaded with me
to help her end her life
even if it meant just wheeling her to the window
so she could tumble out,
her body's last act of grace.
Missing from view, the autopsy scar,
her brain now under a microscope
so they can be certain why her muscles
stopped responding, why when she wanted to walk
her legs folded, when she wanted to breathe
her body stopped. Her eyes are shut,
already turned into the other world
where she can't hear people whisper,
She is better off now.
My mother and I would have looked at each other
and rolled our eyes, as I do now alone,
the morning light oblivious.

SAYING *KADDISH*

for my mother

Even after saying *Kaddish* everyday—
the *yud*, hanging in mid-air,
opening the prayer,
the *tav* silencing the first sound, a breath.
Even after shutting my eyes
and praying with my father
because I want to learn
how to find solace
just chanting the words.
Even after whispering each sound
and then listening to the rain,
then each sound becoming like the rain.
Even after the sun breaks apart the clouds
and in the distance, the thunder,
then the flash of light opening the sky.

OPEN

Calling out to father as he lies in a coma, dying.
Unlike Abraham he didn't know that God would respond.

A cousin wants us to pose behind our fathers'
adjacent graves. *They were so close.*

From mother's deathbed, the drone of soap operas.
Every so often, the *Shema* in whispers.

In the Talmud Rabbi Joshua says, *It is not in heaven.*
The word of God must be determined by men.

The undertaker pulls the rings off mother's fingers.
Her palm opens.

Such is the way of the world: one step at a time,
one word and then the next.

from *Ghosts*, by Paul Auster

EXPOSED

after the painting, *L'Homme et la femme*
by Pierre Bonnard, 1900

Because they just made love late in the afternoon
while Marthe was lying on the bed,
legs slightly apart, posing for him,
Bonnard dashes out from under the covers eager
to get back to work, but he is struck by what he sees
in the mirror: Marthe sitting up now,
reluctant to get out of bed, easily distracted
by the cats that just jumped up
attracted no doubt by the rumpled bedding,
the promise of the warm, moist sheets,
the sour smell of sex. Bonnard looks puzzled
wondering if he can capture the moment
or even if he should: the way Marthe's torso receives
the afternoon light, her hand reaching out
to the cats that are tentative now, their backs lowered
as they step across the covers, purring.

SELF-IMPROVEMENT

On the plane a man writes on a legal pad —
Ten Questions to Ask Yourself.
He closes his eyes for a few seconds
and the page rips itself from the binding,
starts floating through the cabin.
The man tries to retrieve it but can't
and soon everyone tries to catch it.
When they get distracted the page
disappears through the ceiling, fulfilled.

THE MAN IN THE CORPORATE SUIT

He smiles as the wrinkles next to his eyes
become sparrow's feet. He flies
into boardrooms around the world
but the man knows little
about his product, or that it may be killing
children, his children, he knows little
about his children, what they eat for breakfast,
how they argue with mom about
the clothes they wear, what they watch on TV
when they return home from school.
He knows little about mom, she has become
a piece of furniture, or the car,
she has gotten so good at opening and shutting the doors,
buckling the children into their seats.
The man is getting better at his job too,
his boss told him so, sales are up,
he may be in line for the next big promotion
even though he still doesn't know the product
and his kids are eating it, playing with it,
breathing it, even mom is getting into the act
when she doesn't believe she is the car
or when dad flies into the house,
his little heart beating wildly
and the poor man is famished,
he wants his dinner and he wants it now.

REMBRANDT, PETULANT

after the etching, *Self-Portrait, Frowning*
by Rembrandt, 1630

Perhaps the men from the guild decided
not to buy the Rembrandt after all
and chose a Lastman instead,
or Saskia complained once too often
about how cold it is in his Leiden flat
and wouldn't life be better if he had
a proper house in Amsterdam,
so Rembrandt goes into his study and etches his image
into the wax: brows furrowed, lips sealed
to prevent him from saying what he should.
But he was never very good with words,
they always got him into trouble like this morning
when the green grocer tried to sell him
an overripe banana and Rembrandt called him a *klootzak*
so now he won't be able to go in there for days
and Saskia will have to extend his apologies.
Rembrandt continues etching the lines of his forehead,
each one for another man from the guild,
may they all end up at the bottom of a canal.

BIRDWATCHERS IN SILICON VALLEY

A man with a long white beard,
a shirt imprinted with a map
of the ancient world,
and a pair of binoculars
covered in cracked brown leather
dangling from his neck.
He picks them up,
gazes beyond The Wetlands,
oblivious to the rows of concrete buildings
and electrical poles,
a modern history less awesome to him
than the sudden observation
of a blue heron and egret
standing side-by-side.
Look dear, quick, he says,
handing his wife the binoculars,
his clear blue eyes brimming.

FORSAKEN

The former Miss Belgium tells her people
if they elect her into Parliament
she will pose for them in the nude.
The polls say she is favored by a wide margin
and already I can see her first press conference,
TV cameras trained on her breasts
as she condemns NATO's missions into Serbia.
Her breasts become small globes that dissolve into
a map of the Balkans and then we are in Kosovo,
hundreds of refugees crossing the border.
On the wall where the press conference is being held
hangs Bruegel's *Parable of the Blind.*
The sightless men appear to be laughing
as each of them, one by one, stumbles into the river.

AFTER THE MORNING BATH

after the painting, *After the Morning Bath*
by Pierre Bonnard, 1910

It must already be mid-morning
as Marthe gets out of the lukewarm bath
and steps away from the towel
someone is holding like an evening cloak.
The day is just coming into focus:
perhaps she will go to the market
to purchase the foods Pierre loves best—
figs (just in season), camembert,
endives, a freshly killed rabbit.
Or she will tend to the garden, so neglected
since their last trip to Paris—
heaven knows the geraniums need to be cut back,
the roses pruned, the alstroemeria need water.
She turns her head and is struck
by the image in the mirror:
the creases next to her eyes
that Pierre calls his little bird feet
seem deeper, no longer the feet of a sparrow
but those of a crow, and she can hear it
cackling now in the garden, mimicking
every word she is saying to herself—
figs, endives, roses, geraniums—
as she searches for her slippers and notices
how easily her feet slide into the red.

UNSPOKEN

Growing up we rub our open wounds together.
Your words are coursing through my veins.

The lady on six with the numbers branded on her arm,
her apartment always filled with parakeets.

When I am inside you I can feel your heart beat.
The eyes should be off limits while making love.

Marthe exposes Bonnard as he paints her,
the towel waiting to receive her as she steps out of the tub.

Mother waits until I get home.
The undertaker, handing me her wedding band, has no clue.

LAST STATION AT *HAIR CLASSICS*

As the woman from Afghanistan cuts my hair
in Oakland she says, *This is hard for me,*
to touch a man, but she has to do it and then
everything else she has had to do: to open her legs,
her home, to the Russian soldiers and for what,
she cries, *Afghanistan is so poor, I am so poor.*
Her hands glide timidly through my hair
and I imagine her walking through Herat
with her girlfriends, wearing the long black gown,
the veil and looking away when she sees a man
unlike the way she is looking at me now
as she holds a mirror behind my head asking,
Do you like how it looks from the back?
and I see hundreds of pairs of black eyes
piercing me, then slowly turning away.

PUBLIC STORAGE

The woman strolls in with a shopping cart
from Safeway: flowered dresses, torn quilt,
a brown paper bag filled with shoes—
red ones with low heels, black ones, white sandals.
She takes the elevator with us to the second floor,
opens her locker, and pulls out furnishings:
beach chair, small metal table and then
the box of writing—letters, perhaps; stories, poems.
She unfolds the chair, lets down her silver hair
and begins to read. She is quiet for awhile,
then throws back her head, laughs and laughs.
She closes her eyes, the waves lap at her toes,
the sun above her hot, forgiving.

RUSH HOUR

How can it be, the mother scolding
her five-year-old daughter for not listening to her
while the three of them sit on the ground
in the Montgomery Street BART station—
the woman, the girl, the infant—
their red Carl's Junior box filled with loose change.
How can it be, the daughter whimpering, her head lowered
as though her mother had just scolded her
in the living room of their apartment,
the TV blaring the *Six O'Clock News*.
How can it be, the infant wrapped up in a pink blanket,
asleep in her mother's arms,
while the rain drips into a puddle inches from her head.
How can it be, this, the life we have chosen:
to rush home after seeing this,
to walk through the front door,
to sit down at the kitchen table,
to eat. This, after the mother,
with all the strength in her tiny voice:
It's time, Cathy, for a time-out.

THE ONLY JEW IN OSWIECIM

There is only one Jew out of the prewar population of
7,000 still living in Oswiecim (Auschwitz)....
—*N.Y. Times*, June 16, 1998

After the camp was liberated
everyone fled Oswiecim
except those who claimed
they did not know what was going on
when the trains sped through town.
I left too but came back a ghost in hell—
there was no place to flee.
I am Isaac but my story
takes a different ending:
Mt. Moriah is a place in Poland.
Fifty-three years later
people still speak in whispers.

MOON LANDSCAPE

Ilan Ramon took a pencil drawing by a 14-year-old Jewish boy, Peter Ginz, who was killed in Auschwitz.
—*Jewish Virtual Library*

I wonder if he thought about the boy
when he realized the *Columbia*
was malfunctioning,
the boy's drawing of the earth
more fantastic now
than it was in 1942.
The boy called the picture
Moon Landscape
even though it was a drawing
of the earth from the moon,
Theresienstadt not even a speck.

THE CHOSEN

Abraham chose God, then God chose Abraham.
Survivors of Auschwitz speak of an enduring faith.

On a billboard in San Francisco, *Israelis are just like you.*
People walk by turning into mules, tigers, lambs.

The Babylonian Talmud says God kissed Moses on the mouth.
His breath, the language that haunts us.

The *New York Times* notes Daniel Pearl and Nicholas Berg
      were Jewish.
In the *Zohar*, Rabbi Shim'on says Isaac was also being tested.

At a temple in Paris we are frisked before we enter.
The hands of Abraham, perhaps, soothing us.

THE UNSEEN

As the plane begins its descent into San Francisco
in thick cloud cover, the pilot says
And on your left is Yosemite, El Capitán

My mother always hoped that what she had
was Lyme disease so she could give it a name,
imagine that it might be treatable.

The subject in Vermeer's *Woman Reading a Letter*
opens her lover's note quickly, then reads each line over and over
hoping that she might detect a change of heart.

We are compelled by what we can't see
so that we might be surprised
by the things we already know—

The one thought we prey upon,
not unlike the way a bat stalks a grasshopper,
swoops down, then misses.

UNTITLED

A man keeps climbing the Tower of Babel.
That is the only way he can stay out of breath.

A tribe in Africa speaks in clicks.
Sentences are completed by crickets and birds.

Moses had a speech impediment.
His tongue, the handiwork of God.

When our tongues have no need for words.
The eyes can see past the horizon: silence.

The woods are filled with an alphabet of sounds.
After words, we only have wonder.

ABOUT THE AUTHOR

Stewart Florsheim was born in New York City, the son of refugees from Hitler's Germany. He has received several awards for his poetry and has been widely published in magazines and anthologies. He was the editor of *Ghosts of the Holocaust*, an anthology of poetry by children of Holocaust survivors (Wayne State University Press, 1989). He wrote the poetry chapbook, *The Girl Eating Oysters* (2River, 2004). He also writes non-fiction. Stewart's day job is in the technical writing field. He also sits on the board of directors of Compassion and Choices of Northern California, an organization that helps the terminally ill make end-of-life decisions. Stewart lives in the San Francisco Bay Area with his wife, two daughters, and dog.

Printed in the United States